Table of Contents

Executive Summary

Analysis has been a part of American policing for more than a century. Evolving from pin mapping to comparative data tables; from simple patterns analysis and batch processing on mainframe computers to user interface with real-time analysis; and eventually to more flexible and sophisticated analysis, such as the Geographic Information System (GIS), law enforcement has used a variety of analytics to respond to crime. After the terrorist attacks of September 11, 2001, the need for more robust intelligence capabilities and analytic capacity at the state and local law enforcement levels became more apparent than ever before.

Today, the law enforcement analytic function can vary from agency to agency based on the needs of the organization. Whether accomplished by staff analysts who focus on departmental and organizational issues such as budget, policy, and systems, or by line analysts who focus on tactical and strategic analysis for various functions within an agency, effective integration of analysis has been shown to increase law enforcement efficiency and effectiveness in both urban and rural jurisdictions. However, while the benefits of a robust analytic function have been demonstrated through a variety of initiatives, the current economic crisis and the slow rate of change within the policing culture have resulted in an ongoing need to increase analytic capabilities.

Considering the anticipated exponential growth in information and the consequential technology expansion, increased analytic capacity could become the single most-important resource for criminal justice agencies in America. Moving into the next century, agencies should invest in increased analytic capacity to move beyond a world of data analysis of past and current crime trends, and they should incorporate additional factors to efficiently and effectively create a more comprehensive policing strategy.

This report provides an in-depth look at the successful integration of analytics within law enforcement agencies. It examines the application and impact of several initiatives, some of which are based on intelligence-led policing, to include:

- Bureau of Justice Assistance, Targeting Violent Crime Initiative
- Office of Justice Programs, Strategic Approach to Community Safety Initiative
- National Institute for Justice, Study of Law Enforcement Intelligence
- Michigan State University, Intelligence Toolbox Training Program—Intelligence-Led Policing Self-Assessment
- Community-Oriented Policing Services, Integrating Crime Analysis with Patrol Operations

Through the examination of these successful analytic initiatives and in anticipation of the future explosion of the data availability, this report emphasizes the following findings regarding fundamental steps to increase analytic capacity:

- Every law enforcement agency can benefit from developing an analytic capacity.
- Analysts need to have a broad training program to facilitate their ability to fulfill a range of analytic roles within medium-sized and smaller agencies.
- Law enforcement agencies need to develop a professional career track for analysts.
- Medium-sized and smaller agencies need to develop an integrated analytic model to service diverse functions (intelligence analysis, crime analysis, real-time crime, etc.).
- The culture of law enforcement administrators, officers, and elected officials must embrace the value provided by an analyst as a professional member of a law enforcement agency's crime control team.

The Bureau of Justice Assistance, Law Enforcement Forecasting Group offers these recommendations as a means to identify and anticipate problems, forecast crime trends and patterns, allocate agency resources, and prevent or mitigate criminal activity critical to enhancing community safety.

Increasing Analytic Capacity of State and Local Law Enforcement Agencies: Moving Beyond Data Analysis to Create a Vision for Change

Many successful businesses use operations research—the application of specialized analytical methods to help make operational decisions—as a critical component of their business plans to maximize productivity. Theme parks, such as Disney and Universal Studios, use queuing theory to develop the way lines are designed for attractions, to determine how many guests may be serviced at each iteration of the attraction, and to decide how long each attraction iteration should last. National restaurant chains use path and demographic analysis to aid in deciding on locations to build their facilities. Manufacturing businesses, such as Ford and General Motors, use critical path analysis to design the floor plans and sequencing of manufacturing and assembly points. All of these forms of analysis are complex and time-consuming; however, businesses have learned that such analysis is worth the investment to ensure efficiency, effectiveness, quality service delivery, and increased profits. While a wide body of empirical evidence shows that the use of analysis can increase the productivity and effectiveness for all types of organizations, law enforcement has nonetheless been slow to embrace it, particularly as a core management function.

The First Century of Law Enforcement Analytics

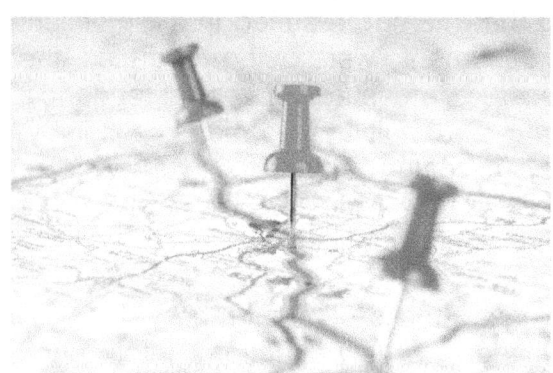

The first documented use of analysis in American policing was in 1906 by August Vollmer, the "father of American policing," in Berkeley, California. Using rudimentary analysis, Vollmer structured patrol beats based on the review of police reports and pin-mapping crimes. His protégé, O. W. Wilson, practiced and advocated further use of analysis in policing in his books *Police Administration*[1] (1950) and *Police Planning*[2] (1957). Stronger and broader recommendations for analysis in law enforcement organizations came from the President's Commission on Law Enforcement and Administration of Justice[3] in 1967, recommending the use of crime analysis, particularly in support of team policing.[4] In the 1970s, crime analysis was a core component of one of the decade's primary crime control initiatives—the Integrated Criminal Apprehension Program.[5] Most of this

---

[1]Wilson, Orlando W. (1950). *Police Administration*. New York: McGraw-Hill Publishing Company.

[2]Wilson, Orlando W. (1957). *Police Planning*. New York: McGraw-Hill Publishing Company.

[3]President's Commission on Law Enforcement and Administration of Justice. (1967). *The Challenge of Crime in a Free Society*. Washington, DC: U.S. Government Printing Office. https://www.ncjrs.gov/pdffiles1/nij/42.pdf

[4]Gay, William, et al. (1976). *Neighborhood Team Policing—National Evaluation Program—Phase 1 Summary Report*. Washington, DC: U.S. Government Printing Office. https://www.ncjrs.gov/app/Search/Abstracts.aspx?id=35296

[5]As an example, see: Greenwood, Peter. (1979). *The RAND Criminal Investigation Study*. Santa Monica, CA: RAND Corporation. http://www.rand.org/pubs/papers/P6352.html

analysis was rudimentary, relying on pin maps, comparative data tables, and some simple patterns analysis. While analysis was employed by some agencies, it was not widespread, being typically limited to major cities, with analysts being largely viewed as clerical workers who did not directly contribute to core policing operations.

As community policing emerged in the 1980s, there was a growing interest in law enforcement for analyzing not only crime trends but also trends in calls for service and community disorder, operating under the theory that eliminating endemic disorder[6] in a community would prevent crime.[7] Changes in technology also aided in more sophisticated analysis. Mainframe computers were transitioning from batch processing systems to individual user interface with real-time analysis, permitting more individualized analysis of crime problems and/or geographic locations. Microcomputing was also emerging. This permitted even more flexible analysis, particularly as Geographic Information System (GIS) software was becoming more readily available.

The community policing philosophy expanded in the late 1980s and 1990s into problem-oriented policing,[8] and the need for analysis became even more prevalent. Expanding further into the CompStat[9] model, more data and GIS requirements were being developed in police departments. Computer technology, more sophisticated software, and the growth of networking, including the Internet, resulted in a significant increase in data and mapping. While mounds of documents were being produced, the quality of the analysis remained largely unsophisticated: measures of central tendency, comparison of tabular data, and multilayered maps. Similarly, analysts were not viewed as being "equal" to sworn officers and consequently were more likely to be viewed as expendable in cases of financial exigency.

Following the terrorist attacks of September 11, 2001, the focus on analysis shifted to a new direction: intelligence analysis for counterterrorism. Law enforcement agencies began developing more robust intelligence capacities, based on guidance from the *National Criminal Intelligence Sharing Plan*[10] and other products of the Global Intelligence Working Group, investments in law enforcement intelligence by the

---

[6]Kelling, George L. and Catherine M. Coles. (1996). *Fixing Broken Windows: Restoring Order and Reducing Crime in our Communities*. New York: Martin Kessler Books.

[7]Carter, David L. (2002). *The Police and the Community*. 7th ed. Englewood Cliffs, NJ: Prentice-Hall, Inc.

[8]Goldstein, Herman. (1990). *Problem-Oriented Policing*. New York: McGraw-Hill Publishing.

[9]Wilson, James, et al. (1990). *CompStat in Practice: An In-Depth Analysis of Three Cities*. Washington, DC: Police Foundation.

[10]http://it.ojp.gov/documents/NCISP_Plan.pdf

U.S. Department of Justice (DOJ) and the U.S. Department of Homeland Security (DHS), and the implementation of state and major urban area fusion centers.

While the increased focus and need for intelligence capacities emerged, the demand for intelligence analysts also increased. However, the law enforcement community was challenged by the limited availability of relevant intelligence analyst training programs. The analyst training programs that were available were offered largely on an ad hoc basis and tended to be of an introductory nature. There were virtually no advanced training programs teaching critical thinking, statistical analysis, or operations research methodologies that could be applied to intelligence analysis. There remains a relative dearth in advanced analyst training.

As state and local law enforcement began developing their intelligence capacities, they began focusing on all crimes, not just terrorism, and the use of intelligence-led policing[11] (ILP) as a driving philosophy of policing.[12] Important, for ILP to be successful, the analytic capacity of the agency must be robust. While evaluation data are relatively limited to this extent, through the evolution and use of law enforcement analysts in previous generations of policing philosophy, some qualitative and quantitative empirical information exists demonstrating the use of analysts as part of the development of ILP.

Beyond operational initiatives, such as ILP, there is an inescapable factor that most law enforcement agencies are currently facing: economic distress. The current economic crisis is having a major impact on agency budgets, often initially addressed by not filling vacant positions, reducing responses to certain types of calls, keeping cars and equipment longer, limiting training, and reducing some services. The economic crisis does not, however, reduce crime or calls for police service—indeed, sometimes the demand increases during economic distress. To overcome the economic handicap, law enforcement needs to work smarter; an effective analytic capacity can provide this by identifying priority threats, providing insight into changes in call demands (both their nature and geographic locations), and enhancing officer responses to handle crimes and calls not only more quickly but also by being armed with better information for decision making. Effective analysis can serve somewhat as a counterbalance to budget reductions. To reinforce this perspective, a recent study of federal, state, and local law enforcement agencies found that hiring for entry-level analysts in support of the law enforcement intelligence function is likely to increase in the near future despite budget reductions.[13]

---

[11]For an historical and developmental discussion of ILP, see: Carter, David L. and Jeremy G. Carter. (2009). *Intelligence-Led Policing: Conceptual and Functional Considerations for Public Policy.* Criminal Justice Policy Review, 20(3), 310–325.

[12] For a detailed discussion of ILP implementation, see: Carter, David L. (2009). *Law Enforcement Intelligence: A Guide for State, Local, and Tribal Law Enforcement Agencies.* 2d. ed. Washington, DC: Office of Community Oriented Policing Services.

[13]Bergendahl, Whitney. (2012). *Entry-Level Hiring Projection for Law Enforcement Intelligence.* Erie, PA: Institute for Intelligence Studies, Mercyhurst College, p. 2.

Perspectives on the Analytic Function

There are different types of analyst positions and different roles an analyst may fill in a law enforcement agency. Broadly defined, there are staff analysts who perform financial analysis of the department's budget; policy analysts who determine the efficacy of current policies and potential alternatives; and systems analysts whose responsibilities are to determine if all components of the law enforcement agency are working at peak efficiencies and are effective in accomplishing organizational goals. There are also line analysts who can be categorized in different ways. They may be classified based on analytic orientation (e.g., tactical or strategic analysis) or by functional responsibility (e.g., crime analyst, intelligence analyst, investigative analyst). Hence, the types and roles of analysts will be dependent on several factors, such as the size of the agency, resources, strategic priorities of the chief executive, and special analytic needs of the agency. Large agencies may be best served by having multiple specialty analysts, while smaller agencies may need a generalist who performs hybrid functions. In reality, the characteristics of the agency, the agency's resources, and the value the chief executive places on the analytic function will drive analytic staffing.

For this paper, the important factor to understand is that management must identify the analytic needs of the agency and then recruit a candidate or candidates who can perform the types of analysis that are needed. There have been some efforts to create national standards for analysts,[14] but more work needs to be done to define educational criteria, skill sets, and performance standards based on the requirements of each "analytic discipline."

Despite the type of analyst, clearly an important skill set for any contemporary law enforcement analyst is the capability to use different technologies. With continuous changes in technology, it is imperative that all analysts be offered continuous training and education. For example, the proliferation of social media has opened a new area that can provide important information about social trends with a criminal nexus as well as identify criminal offenders. Without question, new and innovative technologies and technological applications will emerge that will require continuing education for analysts to develop their expertise.

With respect to expertise, there are sophisticated analytic tools available, such as spatial analytics, artificial intelligence, statistical analytic software, and qualitative analytic tools, all of which can provide the analyst with a wide range of integrated output examining a diverse array of multivariate analyses stratified in many combinations.[15] While these are important and useful tools, they still require critical thinking skills of the analyst to interpret the meaning of the output. These tools can be valuable, particularly when dealing with both large amounts of complex data and a large number of variables, but the output has limited value without skilled interpretation.

---

[14]As one illustration, see: *Law Enforcement Analytic Standards*. (2004). Washington, DC: Global Justice Information Sharing Initiative and the International Association of Law Enforcement Intelligence Analysts.
[15]While there are many such analytic tools currently available on the market, it would be inappropriate to identify specific vendors in this BJA-sponsored paper.

Just as there is an array of analytic tools, there is also a wide range of analytic techniques[16]—both qualitative and quantitative—that are available for the analyst, ranging from the simple (e.g., an association matrix) to the sophisticated (e.g., statistical modeling). The critical factor is to have a trained analyst who can select the proper analytic methodology(ies) to solve the problem or answer the question that is being posed. Similarly, analysts have an important role to "drill down" into the problem, which includes knowing how to ask and answer important questions. Identifying crime hotspots, measuring social trends, developing evidence for criminal liability, determining the effectiveness of a crime control tactic, determining the capabilities and effects of a criminal enterprise, and determining the best financial investment for the purchase of a fleet of police cars are all examples of analytic problems, each requiring a different analytic methodology. To be effective, the analyst must select and employ the methodology that will most accurately answer the question.

Both the analytic tools and techniques are enhanced by the evolution of technology. Analytic, or computational, technology is evolving with processing times getting faster and memory expanding, both at a surprisingly small cost, which in turn means the analyst is able to manipulate larger amounts of data in complex pairings with sophisticated software that can output the results in diverse forms from simple histograms to multilayered color maps. The cumulative impact of tools, techniques, and technology will provide analytic outputs that are more robust and timely. While this will be valuable to the analyst's role, perhaps the more interesting technological developments will be in data-capturing technology: radio frequency identification, smart imaging, the array of diverse sensing technology, and even smartphones. All of these and other emerging data-collection technologies will permit a greater breadth of analysis at micro levels. The result will be more actionable analytic products.

Ideally, the law enforcement agency would develop an internal analytic capacity which would provide a more consistent and timely information flow. In addition, an analyst who is employed by the agency (as a budgeted position, not a grant-supported position) will have a better understanding of the organization, its capabilities, and its challenges, all of which can be particularly important when the analyst makes policy or operational recommendations. In some cases, the nature of a problem or the amount of time required to perform an analysis may require a different organizational model. For example, hiring specialist consultants or partnering with a university or professional organization may provide the most fruitful approach to deal with special or complex analytic problems.

Perhaps one of the greatest challenges in developing a more analytic-driven agency will require organizational change. Reengineering the organization to incorporate an analysis-driven approach will require continuous quality improvement. Just as important, and perhaps the most difficult obstacle, is the resocialization of law

---

[16]As sample illustrations, see: (1) Peterson, Marilyn, et al. (1996). *Successful Law Enforcement Using Analytic Methods*. Richmond, VA: International Association of Law Enforcement Intelligence Analysts.; (2) Carter, David L. (2009). "Chapter 10: Managing Information." *Law Enforcement Intelligence: A Guide for State, Local, and Tribal Law Enforcement Agencies*. 2d ed. Washington, DC: Community Oriented Policing Services Office.

enforcement and government personnel to accept a different approach to policing a community. The image of a uniformed, armed law enforcement officer in a crime-ridden neighborhood is a challenging icon to replace with an analyst; while that is not a practical portrayal, it is the political portrayal that will be used by those who oppose the move to an analytical model. Resocialization will occur when the consumers of analytic products begin seeing increased efficiency and effectiveness of their activities—whether in a line or staff function—as a result of actionable analytic products. With increased appreciation of analytics within police agencies, improvement in capacity will follow.

With successes that have been realized in problem solving, CompStat, evidence-based policing, ILP, and the Smart Policing Initiative, the foundation for an analysis-driven business process has been set in place. For greater success, there must be wider adoption of these practices by law enforcement agencies of all sizes. This requires, for many police and government leaders, rethinking and reengineering police business practices as well as the reallocation of resources to support the analytic functions. Finally, there should be an ongoing evaluation process to ensure the quality and effectiveness of analytic outcomes.

The key points to note are:

- There is a need for an analytic capacity in all agencies.
- There is a critical need for analysts in most medium- to large-sized agencies.
- These analysts must be trained in sophisticated analytic methods and technologies.
- Analysts should be treated by law enforcement organizations—including compensation—as practicing professionals who are critical to the success of the agency's mission.
- Analyst positions should be funded through the budgeting process, not solely through grants.
- Analysts will increase the efficiency and effectiveness of law enforcement operations.

As will be seen, these factors are slowly being experienced.

Current Research and the Growth of an Analytic Capability

There are five sources of data that demonstrate the growth and value of analysis in law enforcement agencies, three of which involve ILP:

- Bureau of Justice Assistance (BJA) Targeting Violent Crime Initiative (TVCI) project site visits
- Office of Justice Programs (OJP) Strategic Approach to Community Safety Initiative (SACSI)
- National Institute of Justice (NIJ) National Study of Law Enforcement Intelligence

- ILP Self-Assessments, as part of a Michigan State University intelligence training program funded by DHS
- Research on the integration of crime analysis with patrol operations, funded by the Office of Community Oriented Policing Services (COPS)

BJA Targeting Violent Crime Initiative (TVCI):

As the intelligence capability of American law enforcement agencies matured, BJA proposed that the lessons learned from ILP could apply to violent crime as well as terrorism. As a result, BJA created the TVCI[17] as a test to see how law enforcement agencies could apply ILP to crimes beyond terrorism. As TVCI-grantee agencies began developing and implementing programs, a number of promising initiatives emerged that had the potential of being replicated in other agencies around the country. In each of these initiatives, the key to success was successful analysis. The following three examples will illustrate the value and application of analysis.

- The City of Richmond, Virginia, was experiencing a significant increase in homicides with clearance rates at an unsatisfactory level. Two factors became clear to police managers— they did not fully understand the nature of these increases, and the department's traditional approach to homicide investigations was not being successful. With a fundamental premise that "If you can't measure it, you can't manage it," the police department began performing a detailed analysis of the homicide 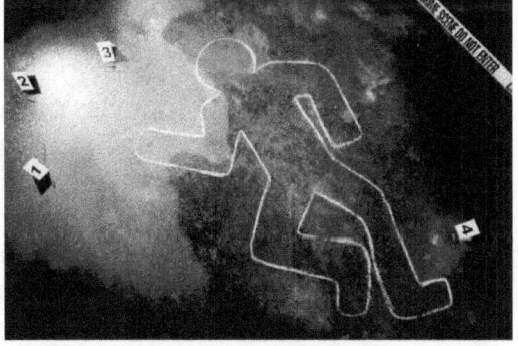 problem in Richmond. The analysis found that the core of the problem appeared to be violence associated with the drug trade, a significant number of which crimes were resulting in homicide. As a result, the homicide investigation function was reengineered, with the first focus being on analysis of crimes. The department developed the Focus Mission Team, which is a proactive crime focus initiative driven by analysts. The analysts work closely with sworn officers and provide high-quality, substantive analysis using diverse analytic tools and mapping in order to better understand crime trends, circumstances of criminal incidents, and forecasts of probable future violence (most notably, retaliation homicides). Stepping beyond the traditional analyst's role, the Richmond Police Department analysts often respond to crime scenes with investigating officers as well as meet with community members. These activities provide new information and context to aid the analysts in providing more robust analytic products. These products are not only used by investigators but also are distributed to patrol officers for the purpose of driving directed patrol based on the findings of the analysis.

---

[17] http://bja.ncjrs.gov/annualreport/2009/chap-6.html

- Evans County, Georgia, is a rural county of 12,000 residents located between Savannah and Macon. The sheriff's office has 12 deputies to not only police the county but to also support the municipal police in two small communities: Claxton, Georgia, with eight police officers, and Hagan, Georgia, with four officers. The motivation for this project was the problems transitioning between the municipalities and the county. Neither the sheriff's office nor the municipal police departments, however, had a good understanding of the ongoing crime problems and the relationships between potential victims and offenders. While there were suspicions and assumptions about the nature of crimes and offenders, the information was not being effectively shared and integrated. The Evans County Sheriff's Office (ECSO) hired an analyst to better understand the crime problems. To facilitate information sharing among agencies within and around Evans County on limited budgets, the ECSO also purchased smartphones for all deputies and municipal officers. Using the smartphones as the method of communications, the analyst pushed intelligence products countywide, including a daily "electronic roll-call briefing." Not only were linkages between crimes and offenders  identified, but the clearance rate for crimes in the county significantly increased. In addition, crimes in neighboring counties were identified and new partnerships were forged, with federal, state, and local law enforcement relying on the products of the ECSO intelligence analyst.

- Although not a TVCI grantee, the Medford, Oregon, Police Department (MPD) effectively incorporated analysis into all aspects of department functions. Medford is a city of 76,860 people located in southwest Oregon just north of the California state line. An upper-income retirement community, the city nevertheless has an unemployment rate of 13 percent and an above-average school dropout rate. Like many other communities, Medford has experienced  a rising gang problem. Prior to initiating a plan for crime control, the MPD conducted an intensive analysis of the community, crime data, and calls for service. Using new knowledge gained from this analysis, patrol beats were realigned and staffing was allocated based on demand. Beyond the use of analysis to reengineer the structure of the police department to meet changes in the community, analysis is used on a regular basis by patrol officers and investigators to address various crime problems. The department's intelligence analysts are proactive, providing a wide range of intelligence products to police personnel. One of the striking aspects of the MPD is how the use of analysis is part of the department's culture. Officers recognized the value analysts provided and consistently sought the analysts' assistance and input on crimes and cases.

There are many other documented successes from the TVCI, demonstrating the value of analysts to law enforcement agencies that are willing to explore new policing models. As these two illustrations show, effective analysis can increase law enforcement efficiency and effectiveness in both urban and rural jurisdictions.[18]

OJP Strategic Approach to Community Safety Initiative (SACSI):

The SACSI exhaustively analyzed the soaring problem of youth homicide and firearms violence in ten cities. SACSI strategies in each city were developed and guided by multiagency, multidisciplinary core groups, with strong and effective leadership provided by U.S. Attorneys' Offices. Each core group included research partners, and data analysis was well integrated into strategic planning and problem solving. The intervention strategies spanned the continuum of enforcement to prevention and were implemented by working groups responsible for day-to-day activities. Successful elements of the SACSI approach include the leadership provided by U.S. Attorneys' Offices, the integration of research, collaborative strategic planning by broad-based core groups, and a range of intervention strategies implemented by working groups. Evidence of the success of "lever-pulling meetings" was mixed, but the deterrent effect of focused suppression efforts was noted.[19] A particularly successful example of the SACSI occurred in Rochester, NY.

Rochester employed a strategic planning process that led to the development and continuous refinement of strategic interventions designed to reduce homicides in the city using a mix of deterrence, incapacitation, and service perspectives. These strategies included changes in prosecution practices, group-focused intelligence gathering, targeted law enforcement efforts, delivery of a deterrence message and service alternative through offender call-ins, intensive supervision of designated probationers, and saturated patrol practices. Evaluation of the overall strategy showed promising results with significant declines in homicides during the 12-month research period, particularly among the target population of young, black males. It is also clear that the SACSI has built on and extended the legacy of collaborative problem solving in criminal justice in Rochester. The collaborative planning process continues under Project Safe Neighborhoods and is also being applied to other problem areas, drug markets in particular. The violence prevention interventions are being institutionalized

---

[18]The case studies of the TVCI will be published in a forthcoming paper: *Reducing Crime Through Intelligence-Led Policing.* (Forthcoming). Washington, DC: Bureau of Justice Assistance, U.S. Department of Justice.

[19]Roehl, Jan, et al. (2006). *Strategic Approaches to Community Safety Initiative (SACSI) in 10 U.S. Cities.* Washington, DC: U.S. Department of Justice. https://www.ncjrs.gov/pdffiles1/nij/grants/212866.pdf

through training in the key criminal justice agencies. Analysts continue to play a significant role in these efforts. Finally, the process in Rochester has served as a model for problem analysis in national training for Project Safe Neighborhoods and is being used by the Division of Criminal Justice Services in New York State as a model for enhancing local analytic capacity and implementing interventions to reduce violence.[20]

NIJ National Study of Law Enforcement Intelligence:

The original project[21] from which these data were gleaned was designed to examine two facets of law enforcement intelligence and information sharing: 1) identify the major obstacles of effective intelligence analysis and information sharing and 2) identify best practices for integrating domestic intelligence into the information sharing environment. The survey was administered to law enforcement personnel who attended the DHS-funded training program "Developing an Intelligence Capacity in State, Local, and Tribal Law Enforcement Agencies."[22] In June 2009, when the survey was disseminated, the program had provided training to 2,395 law enforcement personnel from 1,624 agencies.

The findings indicate that for ILP to be successful, there must be both an understanding of the concept by agency leaders and a commitment to change the organization (including resource reallocation). Of those agencies that had implemented ILP, 87 percent reported that ILP was effective or very effective in crime control.

These findings suggest that familiarity with the ILP concept, including the premise that ILP requires rigorous analysis, can also be interpreted as a recognized need to develop an analytic capability to drive ILP-related operations. The data also suggest that there is a substantial growth in the process to adopt ILP.[23] Collectively, the data suggest that the analytic capability of law enforcement agencies is growing.

Michigan State University, Intelligence Toolbox Training Program—Intelligence-Led Policing Self-Assessment:

As part of a DHS-funded intelligence training program offered nationally over a five-year period, agencies were asked to conduct a self-assessment of their current ILP capacity, including the use of analysts. With respect to the findings, 87 percent of the respondents indicated they worked in a state or local law enforcement agency, with 68 percent indicating their agency had more than 100 sworn personnel. Sixty-four

---

[20]Klofas, John, Christopher Delaney, and Trisha Smith. (2007). *Strategic Approaches to Community Safety Initiative (SACSI) in Rochester, NY*. Washington, DC: National Institute of Justice.

[21]Grant Number 2008-IJ-CX-0007 awarded to the School of Criminal Justice, Michigan State University, School of Criminal Justice in 2009. Co-Principal Investigators: Dr. David Carter, Dr. Edmund McGarrell, and Dr. Steve Chermak.

[22]This training program was developed and delivered by the School of Criminal Justice at Michigan State University through funding provided by the Department of Homeland Security-FEMA Training and Exercise Integration/Training Operations.

[23]For more detailed information on this analysis, see: Carter, Jeremy G. (2011). *Police Innovation: Exploring the Adoption of Intelligence-Led Policing*. A Dissertation. East Lansing, MI: School of Criminal Justice, Michigan State University.

percent of the respondents indicated their agency has at least one intelligence analyst. However, only 48 percent indicated they received valuable strategic intelligence products and 42 percent stated they were provided with valuable tactical intelligence products. When asked if the agency provided officers with relevant actionable intelligence in a timely manner, only 47 percent responded affirmatively.

These data suggest a growing use of analysts by state and local law enforcement agencies. The findings also indicate there is a need for more advanced training and greater direction given to analysts by management on the types of intelligence products that are needed. This leads to an important point: for analysts to provide value to the policing enterprise, not only must analysts be given the skills that are needed to perform their job, but management needs to learn how to best provide direction and use analysts.

Integrating Crime Analysis With Patrol Operations:

The COPS Office funded a national project[24] to develop a guidebook for mid-level managers and commanders of law enforcement agencies who are looking for guidance in fully incorporating crime analysis into their agency, particularly into patrol. Part of this project involved conducting a national survey of 1,000 agencies stratified by agency type, size, and geography. The findings show that 89 percent of the responding agencies employ either a full-time crime analyst or have a staff member whose secondary responsibility is conducting crime analysis. While intuitively this seems to be a high proportion, it is most likely explained by the nature of the sample stratification and the fact that the data include not just full-time analysts but the assignment of some analytic responsibilities to a staff member. The importance of this finding is that responding agencies showed their support for the need and value of analysis in a law enforcement organization.

ILP Research Implications

Collectively, the data suggest that an analyst can provide an important role to a law enforcement agency by:

- Aiding in making complex decisions.
- Helping resolve problems that have inefficient processes.
- Aiding in reducing risk—both risk of crime and management risk.
- Making the greatest use of the data and information collected by the agency.
- Helping to identify new strategies for crime control.
- Helping realign organizational resources to meet crime and call demands.

---

[24]Taylor, Bruce, et al. (2011). *The Integration of Crime Analysis Into Patrol Work: A Guidebook.* Washington, DC: Office of Community Oriented Policing Services, U.S. Department of Justice.

These analytic applications can be seen in two current crime control initiatives where there is ongoing experimentation by law enforcement agencies: the Smart Policing Initiative and real-time crime centers.

Smart Policing Initiative (SPI):

The cumulative experience of law enforcement's use of analysis, particularly as it emerged with CompStat and evolved with intelligence analysis, provided new insights into the applications of analysis for police operations, albeit at a fairly superficial level, particularly when compared to the sophistication of operations research as used in the private sector. This was punctuated with the growth of technology and new common data practices and models, exemplified by the National Information Exchange Model.[25] These factors led BJA to develop the SPI.[26] The SPI seeks to build on the concepts of "offender-based" and "place-based" policing. Several authoritative longitudinal projects have demonstrated that a small number of offenders commit a disproportionate amount of crime. It is also well documented that reports of crime and calls for service often occur predominantly at specific locations or in narrow, easily defined areas. These findings reveal that effective policing requires a tightly focused, collaborative approach that is measurable; based on sound, detailed analysis; and includes policies and procedures to ensure accountability. The SPI aims to either build on these findings or to broaden the knowledge of other effective policing strategies. In addition, this initiative is designed to demonstrate the value of incorporating research, analysis, and the collection of performance measures into the regular strategic thinking and operational planning of law enforcement agencies.[27] Obviously, the role of analysis is a core competency for success.

Real-Time Crime Centers:

Another analytic initiative that is being explored by agencies—New York, Boston, Chicago, Memphis, Philadelphia, and Ogden—is the development of "real-time crime centers." Driven by technological growth, an understanding of the decision-making value of timely comprehensive information sharing, and lessons learned from CompStat and intelligence applications, police leaders are exploring ways to get this information into the hands of patrol officers and investigators as quickly and completely as possible. While there is no singular model, there are three components which appear to be critical: data warehousing, analysis of the data, and a communications mechanism that is fast and preferably has a visual capacity.[28] As noted previously, law enforcement agencies collect massive amounts of information and data. The value of this information is that it can provide important information related to officer safety, crime environments, threats, emerging crime trends, and anomalies of disorder that may be a breeding ground for future crime. The challenge is how to organize, validate, and objectively analyze this information to ensure it is actionable while maintaining privacy

---

[25] http://www.niem.gov
[26] http://www.smartpolicinginitiative.com
[27] http://bja.ncjrs.gov/annualreport/2009/chap-6.html
[28] For example, see: D'Amico, Joseph. (2012). "Stopping Crime in Real Time." *Police Chief Magazine* (January). http://www.policechiefmagazine.org/magazine/index.cfm?fuseaction=display&article_id=995&issue_id=92006

protections. These represent some of the challenges in the new generation of law enforcement information sharing and will necessarily require a skilled analytic capability.

The Next Century of Law Enforcement Analytics

Renowned futurist Ray Kurzweil's law of accelerating returns asserts that the rate of change in technology and other evolutionary systems increases exponentially rather than in a linear fashion. According to Kurzweil:

> An analysis of the history of technology shows that technological change is exponential, contrary to the common-sense "intuitive linear" view. So we won't experience 100 years of progress in the 21st century—it will be more like 20,000 years of progress (at today's rate).[29]

A recent Digital Universe Study found that the world's information is doubling every two years,[30] and many believe that by the year 2020, the amount of information available will double every 73 days.[31] Considering this anticipated exponential growth in information and the consequential technology expansion, increased analytic capacity could become the single most important resource for criminal justice agencies in America.

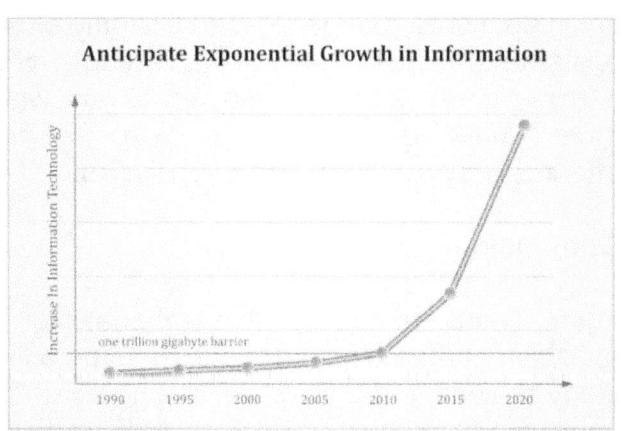

Just as corporate industries have embraced and invested in operations research for their success, criminal justice agencies will need to invest in increased analytic capacity to move beyond a world of data analysis and to efficiently and effectively create a more comprehensive vision for policing. The analytic capacity of law enforcement in the next century must move beyond examination of the past and current crime trends and use of current-day policing techniques; the future of law enforcement analytics must incorporate additional environmental factors, such as projected population, demographics, economics, and technology growth, in order to create a vision and strategy for change.

---

[29] Kurzweil, Ray, "The Law of Accelerating Returns," March 2001. http://www.kurzweilai.net/the-law-of-accelerating-returns

[30] "Extracting Value from Chaos," June 2011, sponsored by EMC. www.emc.com/digital_universe

[31]Appleberry, James B., "Changes in our Future: How Will We Cope?" Faculty speech presented at California State University, Long Beach, California, August 28, 1992.

Training

The role and value of an analyst in law enforcement agencies of all sizes has been demonstrated. An important challenge to be faced is to properly staff analytic positions. The analyst's role in the agency is a professional position that should be staffed by a person who possesses methodological and analytic skills as a result of his or her education and/or experience. These analysts will also need training on crime-specific issues, access and use of proprietary law enforcement networks and systems, legal issues, and processes required in a law enforcement agency.

To maximize the effectiveness of new analysts, a training program needs to be developed and offered on a consistent national basis. The most common training program for state and local law enforcement analysts currently available is the Fundamental Intelligence Analyst Training (FIAT) program. It is a substantively solid program but is actually only a curriculum, not a proprietary program offered by any given sponsor. As a result, FIAT is only offered periodically, is not offered on a national basis, and typically has a variable cadre of instructors. The course is also somewhat narrow, focusing on intelligence analysis, whereas a broader program could address the more expansive role of analysts (e.g., SPI and real-time crime) that could be used more effectively by a wider range of agencies.

Conclusions

There are different types of analysts: crime analysts, intelligence analysts, policy analysts, and systems analysts, to name a few. While the nature of the information they study may vary, the constant among all of these analysts is that they use the scientific approach to problem solving to perform their analysis. The late Carl Sagan, a world-renowned astrophysicist, explained the scientific process this way:

> Science is a way of thinking much more than it is a body of knowledge. Its goal is to find out how the world works, to seek what regularities there may be, to penetrate to the connection of things . . . . Our intuition is by no means an infallible guide. Our perceptions may be distorted by training and prejudice or merely because of the limitations of our sense organs . . . Science is based on experiment, on a willingness to challenge old dogma, on an openness to see the universe as it really is . . . . If you spend any time spinning hypotheses, checking to see whether they make sense, whether they conform to what else we know, thinking of tests you can pose to substantiate or deflate your hypotheses, you will find yourself doing science.[32]

---

[32]Sagan, Carl. (1979). *Broca's Brain: Reflections on the Romance of Science.* New York: The Ballantine Publishing Group.

It is the analyst who applies the scientific method to draw meaning from the data and information that is collected by a law enforcement agency. In making observations about data collection in policing, the RAND Corporation's study *Moving Toward the Future of Policing* observed:

> The massive increase in data collection and storage capability has resulted in an enormous increase in the amount of available information to which police organizations have access when trying to combat crime. Yet, without appropriate tools for organizing, managing, and sifting through these massive amounts of data, the data may drown police, not help them. All that data may do nothing more than require multiple times more man-hours for personnel to cull through the haystacks of data, looking for the needle. More data could simply mean more work, not smarter or more effective policing.[33]

In order to understand the implications from this mass of data, trained analysts will be increasingly needed. The analyst can convert these "haystacks of data" into meaningful new knowledge on which management and operational decisions may be made. RAND goes on to observe that:

> . . . advances that change the ways in which police departments gather, process, share, and protect data and information are going to have increasingly profound impacts on police organizations. Organizations will become more networked and systems-oriented in a shift toward data-driven policing.[34]

It is the essential role of a trained analyst that is going to drive this type of organizational change. To begin this process, there are fundamental steps which need to be addressed:

- Every law enforcement agency, regardless of size, can benefit from developing an analytic capacity.
- Analysts need to have a broad training program to facilitate their ability to fulfill a range of analytic roles within medium-sized and smaller agencies.
- Law enforcement agencies need to develop a professional career track for analysts.
- Medium-sized and smaller agencies need to develop an integrated analytic model to service diverse functions (intelligence analysis, crime analysis, real-time crime, etc.).

---

[33]Trevorton, Gregory, et al. (2011). *Moving Toward the Future of Policing*. Santa Monica, CA: RAND Corporation. p. 78.
[34]Ibid. p. 88.

A final challenge is changing the culture of law enforcement administrators, officers, and elected officials to understand the value provided by an analyst as a professional member of a law enforcement agency's crime control team. Proactive policing strategies that rely upon data and analysis as a method to identify and anticipate problems, forecast crime trends and patterns, allocate agency resources, and prevent or mitigate criminal activity are critical to enhancing community safety.

Appendix A

Law Enforcement Forecasting Group Members

<u>Law Enforcement Forecasting Group Members</u>

Sheriff John Cary Bittick
Monroe County, Georgia, Sheriff's Office

Brenda Bond, Ph.D.
Suffolk University

Chief Jim Bueermann (Retired)
Redlands, California, Police Department

Bob Bushman
Minnesota Department of Public Safety

Chief Jane Castor
Tampa, Florida, Police Department

James Coldren, Ph.D.
Governors State University

Deputy Commissioner Nola Joyce
Philadelphia, Pennsylvania, Police Department

Colonel Steven McCraw
Texas Department of Public Safety

Chief Walter McNeil
Quincy, Florida, Police Department

Assistant Sheriff Ted Moody
Las Vegas, Nevada, Metropolitan Police Department

Interim Chief Randy Schoen
Sutherlin, Oregon, Police Department

Chief Ray Schultz
Albuquerque, New Mexico, Police Department

Larry Travis, Ph.D.
University of Cincinnati

Michael Wagers, Ph.D.
International Association of Chiefs of Police